THIS BOOK BELONGS TO:

_____

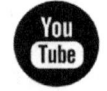 DRAWING WITH DREW

All rights reserved. This material cannot be reproduced without permission from the creator.

Copyright © 2017 Andrew Tyers
All rights reserved.
ISBN10: 1977612938
ISBN-13: 978-1977612939

1. YOU'RE VISITING AN ANIMAL RESERVE IN TAIWAN. A CURIOUS MONKEY TAKES SOMETHING FROM YOUR BAG. WHAT IS IT?

2. YOU'VE DONATED YOUR BODY TO AN EXPERIMENTAL SCIENCE PROGRAM. DRAW YOURSELF AFTER THE SCIENTISTS HAVE COMPLETED THE OPERATION.

3. YOU'VE JUST WALKED THROUGH A WORMHOLE. IT'S NOW THE YEAR 2099. DRAW WHAT YOU SEE.

4. YOU'VE JUST ORDERED "THE SPECIAL" AT A DODGY BACK-ALLEY RESTAURANT. DRAW WHAT'S ON YOUR PLATE.

5. YOUR WORST NIGHTMARE JUST CAME TRUE. DRAW IT.

6. THIS MACHINE IS POWERED ENTIRELY BY STEAM. IT ALSO HAS A VERY SPECIAL FUNCTION. DRAW IT.

7. THINK OF YOUR GREATEST ATTRIBUTE. NOW DRAW YOURSELF AS A SUPERHERO, ACCENTUATING THIS ENHANCED ABILITY.

8. THE WATER WON'T GO DOWN YOUR KITCHEN SINK. IT'S PLUGGED. WHAT'S BLOCKING THE DRAIN?

9. AN EMERGENCY NEWS REPORT STATES THAT A CRAZED CLOWN IS ON THE LOOSE. DRAW THE CLOWN.

10. IT'S THE LAST DAY ON EARTH. DRAW WHAT YOU ARE DOING.

11. WHAT IS LOVE? DRAW IT.

12. YOU JUST GRADUATED FROM THE MOST PRESTIGIOUS COLLEGE OF WIZARDRY. DRAW YOURSELF.

13. YOU WALK DOWN THE STEPS TO THE OLDEST BAKERY IN FRANCE. YOU OPEN THE DOOR. DRAW THE INSIDE OF THE BAKERY.

14. DRAW A CREATURE EATING ANOTHER CREATURE.

15. THE MOST DELICIOUS CUPCAKE THIS WORLD HAS EVER TASTED.

16. IT'S 5:30 A.M. YOU ARE AWOKEN BY THE SOUND OF THUMPING. YOU FIND YOUR NEIGHBOUR BURYING SOMETHING IN YOUR BACKYARD. DRAW IT.

17. A DOOR-TO-DOOR SALESMAN FINISHES A LONG DAY WITH NO SALES. DRAW HIM.

18. SANTA CLAUS'S HALF-BROTHER, STEVE, HAS COME TO TAKE OVER SANTA'S WORKSHOP. DRAW THEIR INTERACTION.

19. THIS CARROT IS CONSCIOUS AND MISCHIEVOUS.

20. YOU HAVE BEEN REINCARNATED INTO SOMETHING OF YOUR CHOOSING. WHAT HAVE YOU BECOME?

21. THIS GUY JUST WON FIRST PRIZE AT A BEARD AND MOUSTACHE COMPETITION.

22. YOU'RE SPENDING THE NIGHT IN YOUR CAR WITH YOUR BEST FRIEND. DRAW THE SCENE INSIDE YOUR CAR.

23. A DEADLY WEAPON.

24. THIS GIRL JUST FINISHED TWO WEEKS AT SUMMER CAMP. DRAW HER.

25. YOU ASK TO USE THE BATHROOM IN A BACK-ALLEY CONVENIENCE STORE. THIS IS WHAT YOU FIND.

26. YOU'RE ON A FISHING TRIP WITH THE WHOLE FAMILY. YOU WEREN'T EXPECTING TO CATCH THIS.

27. YOU'RE HIKING THROUGH THE PERUVIAN JUNGLE AND STUMBLE UPON AN ABORIGINAL TRIBE. THEY THINK YOU ARE THEIR GOD. DRAW YOURSELF AS THEIR LEADER.

28. INSIDE GRANDMA'S LIVING ROOM ON A FRIDAY NIGHT AT 11:00 P.M.

29. YOU'VE JUST WON THE EMPLOYEE OF THE MONTH AWARD AT YOUR LOCAL BURGER JOINT. DRAW THE PHOTO OF YOU THAT THEY HANG ON THE WALL.

30. THIS ASTRONAUT IS INSIDE A ROCKET SHIP ORBITING THE EARTH.

31. THIS CARNIVAL RIDE OPERATOR HAS SEEN BETTER DAYS.

32. THIS CAR IS AN 'OLDIE BUT A GOODIE.'

33. YOUR FAVOURITE CHILDHOOD TOY.

34. A MYSTICAL FAIRY WAKES YOU IN THE NIGHT TO TELL YOU A SECRET. DRAW THE FAIRY.

35. THERE IS SOMETHING STRANGE ABOUT THE GUY SITTING ACROSS FROM YOU ON THE BUS. WHAT DOES HE LOOK LIKE?

36. AN ARTIFACT FOUND IN AN OLD, ABANDONED MINE.

37. YOUR PROUDEST MOMENT.

38. AN INTRIGUING DONUT.

39. IT'S DINNER TIME IN PRISON. YOU LOOK DOWN AT YOUR TRAY. DRAW EACH ITEM.

40. IMAGINE THERE IS A SPIDER LIVING IN THE CORNER OF YOUR BEDROOM. DRAW WHAT IT SEES.

41. IT HAS BEEN 48 HOURS SINCE A MAJOR GLOBAL CATASTROPHE. YOU SURVIVED. WHAT ARE YOU DOING?

42. THIS DETAILED MAP SHOWS THE LOCATION OF WHERE SOMETHING SPECIAL IS HIDDEN.

43. THIS PIECE OF PIE HAS A VERY UNUSUAL FILLING.

44. YOU ARE STANDING ON TOP OF A GIANT GINGERBREAD HOUSE LOOKING OUT OVER A LAND MADE OF CANDY AND SWEETS.

45. AN EERIE YET BEAUTIFUL VISTA.

46. AN EXOTIC DELICACY FROM A FAR OFF LAND.

47. THIS SILLY TORTOISE TELLS JOKES.

48. THIS BUSINESS WOMAN JUST EARNED A HUGE COMMISSION FOR LANDING A CORPORATE CLIENT. DRAW HER.

49. THE DOG'S BEEN INTO THE GARBAGE AGAIN! DRAW THE SCENE.

50. IT'S RUSH HOUR. DRAW YOURSELF AT THE BUSIEST SUBWAY STATION IN JAPAN.

51. DRAW THE UGLIEST SWEATER YOU HAVE EVER SEEN.

52. THESE HAVE GOT TO BE THE COOLEST SHOES OF ALL TIME. DRAW THEM.

53. A HALF ANIMAL, HALF HUMAN CREATURE THAT LIVES IN THE ATTIC.

54. A DISEASE IS SPREADING THROUGH THE POPULATION. DRAW A MUTANT CHILD.

55. THIS GUY TAKES AN ABSURD AMOUNT OF STEROIDS.

56. YOU ARE ALONE FOR THE WEEKEND. DRAW WHAT YOU'RE DOING.

57. IF YOU GET YOUR PICTURE TAKEN WITH THIS EVIL CAMERA, IT CAPTURES YOUR SOUL.

58. YOU FALL ASLEEP IN A BOAT ONLY TO AWAKEN IN THE MIDDLE OF THE OCEAN. DRAW THE SCENE.

59. THIS SPACE TRAVELLER SOLVES PROBLEMS ON ALIEN PLANETS. DRAW THE TRAVELLER.

60. DRAW THE MERMAID THAT JUST SAVED YOU FROM DROWNING.

61. THIS CONTAINER HOLDS THE LIQUID TO ETERNAL LIFE.

62. A DELICIOUS, ARTERY CLOGGING, SLICE OF PIZZA.

63. AN EVIL THOUGHT.

64. AN OBJECT ON DISPLAY IN A DOCTOR'S HOUSE.

65. THIS IS JEALOUSY.

66. YOU WON'T SEE THIS SUPERHERO IN ANY MAINSTREAM COMIC BOOK.

67. DRAW AN INVESTIGATIVE CRIME SCENE AFTER AN EVENT HAS TAKEN PLACE.

68. DRAW HAPPINESS.

69. YOUR SCHOOL PHOTO FROM A LONG TIME AGO.

70. THE TROPHY YOU RECEIVED FROM PARTICIPATING IN AN OBSCURE EVENT.

71. THIS CREATURE EATS CATS.

72. YOU'RE A DOG WALKING THROUGH A PARK. DRAW WHAT YOU SEE FROM YOUR PERSPECTIVE.

73. THIS GUY PLAYS COMPUTER GAMES FROM 6:00 P.M. UNTIL 4:00 A.M. EVERY DAY. DRAW HIM.

74. YOU'RE AT A PARTY. YOU LOOK AT THE PERSON TO YOUR LEFT. THEY TOTALLY OVERDRESSED FOR THE OCCASION. DRAW WHAT THEY ARE WEARING.

75. THIS PERSON FAR EXCEEDS THE WEIGHT RESTRICTIONS TO RIDE ON THE ROLLER COASTER. THEY RIDE IT ANYWAY. DRAW THE SCENE.

76. THIS FOOT IS IN REALLY ROUGH SHAPE.

77. THIS INNOCENT LOOKING OLD LADY STEALS.

78. YOU'RE AT A COFFEE SHOP. THE HIPSTER NEXT TO YOU JUST BURNED THE CRAP OUT OF HIS TONGUE. DRAW THE SCENE.

79. THE PET YOU'RE HIDING IN YOUR BASEMENT COMES FROM ANOTHER PLANET. DRAW IT.

80. DESIGN A BOX OF UNHEALTHY CEREAL FOR KIDS.

81. AN OLD SKATEBOARDING LEGEND.

82. THIS WOMAN IS DISPROPORTIONATELY FIGURED.

83. DRAW THE INSIDE OF YOUR REFRIGERATOR. DON'T FORGET THE CONDIMENTS.

84. YOU REACH INTO THE INSIDE POCKET OF YOUR OLD JACKET. THAT'S WHERE YOU PUT IT! DRAW THE OBJECT.

85. A CHILDHOOD BULLY.

86. THIS PUNK KID VANDALIZES PROPERTY FOR FUN.

87. DRAW A HOUSE COVERED IN WHIMSICAL VEGETATION.

88. THAT KID HAS A FLATULENCE PROBLEM.

89. It's a special occasion. Your family has agreed to go to a professional photographer to get a high-quality photo of everyone. Draw your family.

90. YOU FIND A SEED IN YOUR GREAT GRANDPARENTS' HOUSE. YOU PLANT IT. IT GROWS INTO A PLANT THOUGHT TO HAVE GONE EXTINCT 300 YEARS AGO. DRAW THE PLANT.

91. THIS GUY WEARS A CAPE.

92. YOU JUST FINISHED EATING THE SPICIEST HOT PEPPER IN THE WORLD. THIS IS WHAT YOUR FACE LOOKS LIKE IMMEDIATELY AFTERWARD.

93. THIS COLLEGE STUDENT IS ADDICTED TO CAFFEINATED BEVERAGES.

94. AN OCTOPUS AND A SHARK HAD OFFSPRING. DRAW THIS NEW CREATURE.

95. THIS GUY JUST LOST HIS ENTIRE MONTH'S RENT AT THE CASINO.

96. THIS INVENTION WAS USED IN THE 1920'S TO MAKE PEOPLE SMARTER.

97. DRAW A VEHICLE THAT RESEMBLES A TYPE OF FOOD.

98. YOUR OVERWEIGHT, ADULT NEIGHBOUR HAS DECIDED TO TAKE A DIP IN A CHILD-SIZED SWIMMING POOL ON THEIR FRONT LAWN.

99. THIS BIRD JUST POOPED ON YOUR FRESHLY-WASHED CAR.

100. DRAW THE INSIDE OF A SCIENTIST'S LABORATORY IN THE EARLY 1900S.

101. A SHELF OF INGREDIENTS IN A WITCH'S KITCHEN.

102. THIS KID GOT HIT IN THE FACE WITH A BASKETBALL. HE'S HAVING A TERRIBLE, UNCONTROLLABLE NOSE BLEED.

103.   DRAW SOMETHING THAT FRIGHTENS YOU.

104.   THIS GUY LIVES IN THE SEWER.

105.   THESE GUYS USE HELIUM BALLOONS INSTEAD OF A CLOTHESLINE TO DRY THEIR LAUNDRY.

106. A WELL-LOVED DOG TOY.

107. DRAW A HAND THAT HAS FACIAL FEATURES.

108. YOUR PET RAT HAS A SPECIAL ABILITY. WHAT IS IT?

109. DRAW YOURSELF 10 YEARS FROM NOW. WHAT ARE YOU DOING?

110. A MYSTERIOUS MAN GIVES YOU AN AMULET. DRAW THE AMULET.

111. THIS BIZARRE PAINTING WAS PAINTED BY AN OLD MASTER AND IS WORTH A FORTUNE.

112. YOU'RE USING A METAL-DETECTOR ON A BEACH IN THE CARIBBEAN. YOU FIND A COIN THAT MOST LIKELY CAME FROM AN OLD PIRATE SHIP. DRAW IT.

113. DRAW YOUR ALTER-EGO.

114. THE INSIDE OF A BANK WITH A ROBBERY IN PROGRESS.

115.   A VINTAGE COMPUTER COVERED IN STICKERS.

116.   THIS PIECE OF MEDICAL EQUIPMENT WAS USED TO FLUSH THE TOXINS FROM ONE'S BODY IN THE 1800'S.

117. A COMMANDO SLUG CAPABLE OF UTTER DESTRUCTION.

118. THIS MONSTER LIVES IN YOUR CLOSET AND LICKS THE BOTTOM OF YOUR SHOES.

119. A DEMENTED TOOTH FAIRY IN MID FLIGHT.

120. YOUR FRIEND HAS SOMETHING ON HER NECK. DRAW IT.

121. THE MAID AT A CARIBBEAN RESORT WAS CAUGHT DOING SOMETHING SHE SHOULDN'T HAVE BEEN DOING.

122. A PIECE OF SPACE JUNK FLOATING AROUND THE ATMOSPHERE.

123. PEERING FROM BEHIND A BUSH, YOU SEE THIS OBJECT FLOATING IN A SWAMP.

124. HEARING A JOKE SO FUNNY THAT YOU PUKE.

125. A SMALL SNIPPET OF A CITY DIRECTLY FOLLOWING THE AFTERMATH OF A TSUNAMI.

126. THIS ENCHANTED MUSICAL INSTRUMENT CAUSES YOU TO GO DEAF.

127. SKETCH YOUR FAVOURITE THING THAT HAPPENED THIS WEEK.

128. AN INCONSIDERATE GESTURE.

129.   A WARLOCK'S CAULDRON FULL OF BIZARRE INGREDIENTS.

130.   THIS DISGRUNTLED GOVERNMENT EMPLOYEE JUST REACHED HER BOILING POINT.

131. THIS IS WHAT YOUR ARCH ENEMY WOULD LOOK LIKE.

132. DRAW A ZOMBIE'S HAND. INCLUDE WHAT IT'S HOLDING.

133. AN INSANE MENTAL PATIENT IS LOOSE ON THE STREETS.

134.   THIS WIZARD'S SPELL WENT HORRIBLY WRONG.

135.   THIS CELLPHONE DOES MUCH MORE THAN JUST MAKE CALLS. IT ALSO HAS A HIDDEN FEATURE.

136. You're on a nature tour in the middle of the Amazon rainforest. Your vehicle breaks down. Draw the situation.

137. You are looking at the movie poster for an upcoming film you'd like to see. Sketch the poster.

138. Draw a villain that would be used in a child's cartoon series.

139. THIS LIL' FELLA LIVES UP IN A TREE HOUSE WITH OTHERS LIKE HIM.

140. THIS IS WHAT A TOASTER FROM THE FUTURE LOOKS LIKE.

141. THIS CAT IS ON ITS NINTH LIFE.

142. THIS DENTIST HAS A CRIMINAL OFFENSE ON HIS RECORD. DRAW WHAT HE LOOKS LIKE.

143. THIS BRIDGE LEADS TO A CASTLE IN THE MOUNTAINS. DRAW THE SCENE.

144. THIS IS WHAT YOU LOOK LIKE AT 6:00 A.M.

145. A STRANGE ALIEN ENCOUNTER LEFT THIS SHEEP LOOKING...PECULIAR.

146.   A FUTURISTIC MOTORCYCLE.

147.   DRAW THE BIKER THAT JUST WHOOPED YOUR BUTT AT POOL.

148. A WOMAN ESCAPING FROM A 2ND STORY WINDOW IN CHINA TOWN.

149. DRAW THE LADY THAT OPERATES THE RING TOSS STATION AT A CARNIVAL.

150. AN IMMORTAL KING SENT DOWN FROM THE HEAVENS.

151. THIS THING WAS AT THE BOTTOM OF YOUR COFFEE CUP.

152. DRAW THE NEXT POINT OF HUMAN EVOLUTION. WHAT WILL OUR SPECIES LOOK LIKE?

153. THIS GUY HAS BEEN LIVING ALONE IN THE WOODS FOR WAY TOO LONG.

154. THIS OLD WOMAN MAKES PIES OUT OF FROGS AND FISH GUTS.

155. THE FACE OF A GUY WHO EATS FAST FOOD AT EVERY MEAL.

156.   IT'S YOUR 21ST BIRTHDAY. YOUR FRIENDS GET YOU A GIANT CAKE. SKETCH WHAT'S INSIDE.

157.   THIS ENCHANTED SOUL IS DOOMED TO WANDER THE CEMETERY FOR ALL OF ETERNITY.

158. YOU WEREN'T EXPECTING TO SEE THIS STRANGE ANIMAL AT THE ZOO. IT LOOKS LIKE A FEW ANIMALS FUSED INTO ONE.

159. A HIGH SCHOOL DROPOUT.

160.   DRAW A SHARK DEVOURING A SURFER.

161. THIS PERSON HAS AN EXTREMELY CONTAGIOUS DISEASE.

162. YOU ARE A COMIC BOOK COLLECTOR. YOU'VE JUST STUMBLED UPON A RARE COMIC WORTH A FORTUNE. DRAW THE FRONT COVER OF THE COMIC BOOK.

163. AN ICE CREAM CONE ON A HOT SUMMER DAY.

164. THIS IS THE JACKET YOU WEAR WHEN EMBARKING ON INTERPLANETARY TRAVEL.

165.   A SNAKE EATING A JUICY RAT.

166.   DRAW THE ANNOYING GUY WHO HAS AN ANSWER FOR EVERYTHING.

167.   YOU'RE ON THE ROOF OF A 30-STORY BUILDING.
    THIS IS WHAT YOU'RE DOING.

168. Draw a humongous giant crushing a tiny town.

169. YOU AND YOUR FAMILY CAREFULLY GATHER AROUND AN EGG THAT IS READY TO HATCH. THIS CAME OUT.

170. THIS BOTTLE OF HOT SAUCE IS GUARANTEED TO CAUSE ACID REFLUX. DRAW THE BOTTLE/LABEL.

171. THE MOST INCREDIBLE TATTOO YOU'VE EVER SEEN ON SOMEONE'S FACE.

172. DRAW WHAT THE EASTER BUNNY LOOKS LIKE DURING ITS TIME OFF.

173. MEET TONY AND HIS GOONS.

174.   AN AGGRESSIVE, UNCONTROLLABLE SNEEZE.

175.   YOU AND YOUR BEST FRIEND SET OFF ON A BACKPACKING TRIP AROUND THE WORLD. THIS IS THE PHOTOGRAPH THAT WAS TAKEN OF YOU WITH ALL YOUR GEAR.

176. An obese guy beside you on the plane has fallen asleep on your shoulder. Draw the scene.

177. Draw an intricate marble maze that works using gravity.

178. UNICORN MEAT BEING SOLD ON THE STREETS OF BANGKOK. DRAW THE SITUATION.

179. THIS MACHINE GIVES AUTOMATIC HAIRCUTS.

180. DRAW A PICTURE OF YOURSELF WEARING YOUR FAVOURITE OUTFIT. INCLUDE ACCESSORIES.

181.   DRAW A DAY IN YOUR LIFE.

182.   YOUR FRIEND IS CELEBRATING HER BIRTHDAY AT A LOCAL PUB. YOU'RE UNDER-AGE. LUCKILY FOR YOU, YOU HAVE A FAKE ID. DRAW IT.

183.   YOU'RE STOPPED AT A RED LIGHT. THE PEOPLE IN THE CAR NEXT TO YOU ARE DOING THIS.

184. IT'S SO UGLY IT'S CUTE.

185. WARNING: DRINKING TOXIC SLUDGE MAY CAUSE ABNORMALITIES. WHAT ARE THEY?

186. THIS NEAR-SIGHTED BIRD ISN'T SITTING ON ITS EGGS. WHAT IS IT KEEPING WARM?

187. YOU JUST MADE UP A NEW MARTIAL ARTS MOVE. THIS IS WHAT IT LOOKS LIKE.

188. A SLOPPY BURGER WITH ALL THE FIXINGS.

189. A BEJEWELED SKULL SITTING ON TOP OF AN ANCIENT PEDESTAL.

190.   AN OLD-TIMEY HORSE AND BUGGY, TRANSPORTING A VERY IMPORTANT PERSON.

191. A HELICOPTER RIDE THAT YOU WILL NEVER FORGET.

192. YOU'VE CORNERED THE THIEF THAT JUST PICKED YOUR POCKET. DRAW WHAT HE LOOKS LIKE.

193. THIS WOMAN HAS 11 PET CATS. THEY AREN'T ALLOWED OUTSIDE. DRAW HER APARTMENT.

194. YOU HOVER OVER A TOILET IN A GAS STATION RESTROOM. NO TOILET PAPER! THIS IS WHAT YOUR FACE LOOKS LIKE.

195. THIS GUY MAY NOT LOOK LIKE YOUR TYPICAL HOLLYWOOD HUNK, BUT LADIES ADORE HIM ALL THE SAME.

196.   DRAW YOUR DREAM DATE.

197.   THIS LASER TURNS THINGS TO VAPOR.

198.   AN ATOM BOMB, THE SIZE OF DELAWARE, DETONATES. DRAW THE VIEW FROM SPACE.

199.   DRAW SOMETHING STINKY.

200. THIS CHICK WON FIRST PRIZE AT AN UNUSUAL BEAUTY PAGEANT.

201. YOU'RE AT A HOT YOGA CLASS AND THE INSTRUCTOR PUSHES YOU A LITTLE TOO FAR. THIS IS WHAT HAPPENS.

202.   A JAR OF SOMETHING PICKLED.

203.   QUEEN IZABELLA LOOKS SWEET BUT HAS BEEN KNOWN TO BEHEAD HER ENEMIES.

204. THIS KID JUST ATE HIS/HER ENTIRE BAG OF HALLOWE'EN CANDY IN ONE SITTING.

205. THIS WOOLLY MAMMOTH WAS CREATED IN A LABORATORY.

206. SOMETHING JUST BIT YOU. WHAT WAS IT?

207. A GIANT OGRE USED A COTTON SWAB TO CLEAN OUT ITS EAR. DRAW ALL THE STRANGE ITEMS LODGED IN THE EAR WAX.

208. THIS BIZARRE CREATURE IS YOUR PRIMARY MODE OF TRANSPORTATION. DRAW IT.

209. A BUCKET FULL OF GREASY, CRISPY CHICKEN.

210. YOU'RE AT A WORLD RENOWNED MAGIC SHOW. DRAW ONE OF THE MAGIC PROPS ON STAGE.

211. YOU ACCIDENTLY DROPPED YOUR ROLEX IN THE MAILBOX. YOU REACH IN TO RETRIEVE IT, ONLY TO GET STUCK! DRAW THE SCENE.

212. NOT YOUR TYPICAL CRIME FIGHTING DUO.

213. THE STRANGEST SANDWICH YOU HAVE EVER EATEN.

214. THESE HORS D'OEUVRES WERE SERVED AT YOUR UNCLE'S WEDDING. THEY ARE STILL ALIVE.

215. STUFFING YOUR FACE AT AN ALL-YOU-CAN-EAT RESTAURANT.

216. YOU GIVE THIS STRAY DOG A MUCH NEEDED WASH IN YOUR BATHTUB. DRAW THE SCENE.

217. THE MOST ANNOYING PART OF YOUR DAY.

218. A LITTLE PRESENT FOR YOUR BOSS.

219. THIS COUPLE HAS BEEN MARRIED FOR 67 YEARS.

220. WHAT LOOKS LIKE A WEIRD MOLE IS GROWING ON YOUR KNEE CAP. UPON CLOSER INSPECTION, YOU REALIZE IT'S SOMETHING ELSE. DRAW WHAT YOU SEE.

221. THIS DOCTOR PERFORMS SURGERY IN AN OLD, WINE CELLAR.

222. THIS SEAGULL HAS SOMETHING CAUGHT IN ITS BEAK. DRAW IT.

223. THE QUEEN OF THE FROGS.

224. YOU SMUGGLED THIS DELICIOUS TREAT INTO FAT CAMP. DRAW IT.

225. THIS FORTUNE TELLER HAS A MORBID SENSE OF HUMOUR. DRAW HER.

226. THESE GUYS HAVE BEEN FOLLOWING YOU ALL DAY.

227. DRAW A PICTURE OF A STEREOTYPICAL NERD.

228.   AN OVERWORKED NURSE.

229.   THIS BOAT IS BEING CONSUMED BY AN EXTRAORDINARY SEA CREATURE.

230.   A CLUTTERED CLOSET.

231. YOU'RE HAVING GUT PAIN. A SCAN REVEALS A VERY UNUSUAL OBJECT LODGED IN YOUR STOMACH. DRAW WHAT THE X-RAY REVEALS.

232. YOU'RE IN A LONG LINE FOR THE BATHROOM. SKETCH THE PEOPLE IN THE LINE.

233. THE HEAD CUSTODIAN AT A HIGH SCHOOL.

234. THIS ANTIQUE LOCKET HOLDS PICTURES OF TWO LOVERS.

235. A MECHANIC WORKING ON A JUNKER.

236. THE ANSWER TO ALL OF LIFE'S PROBLEMS.

237. HAVING A SPIRITUAL EXPERIENCE.

238. THIS TAXI DRIVER DOESN'T SPEAK YOUR LANGUAGE.

239. THIS LITTLE KID JUST POOPED IN THEIR FULL-BODY SNOW SUIT.

240. IF YOU COULD BE DOING ANYTHING YOU WANTED THIS VERY INSTANT, WHAT WOULD IT BE? DRAW YOURSELF THERE.

241. YOU'RE IN AN OLD PHONE BOOTH IN AN EERIE PART OF TOWN. THERE ARE BUSINESS CARDS ALL OVER THE GROUND. YOU PICK ONE UP WITH A PICTURE ON IT. SKETCH THE CARD.

242.   A THUMP AT YOUR WINDOW. WHAT FELL TO THE GROUND?

243.   DRAW LONELINESS.

244. THIS PLANT HAS CARNIVOROUS TENDENCIES.

245. THIS GUY LOOKS LIKE HE'S BEEN HIT BY A TRUCK.

246. YOUR IDEA OF THE BEST PARENTS IN THE WORLD.

247. A REALISTIC-LOOKING FACE.

248.   A BOAT IN A BOTTLE.

249.   AN OLD PHOTOGRAPH OF SOMEONE YOU DON'T KNOW.

250.   AN OLD EUROPEAN MAN SUNBATHING ON A BEACH.

251.   THE SICKEST TREEHOUSE YOU HAVE EVER SEEN.

252. THIS PIG'S BEEN STUFFED AND IS READY FOR ROASTING.

253. THIS MAN ONLY SHAVED HALF OF HIS FACE AND HAIR.

254. A WEDDING CAKE HITTING THE GROUND.

255. POLICE UNIFORMS OF THE FUTURE.

256.   A FLOATING CITY IN THE SKY.

257. THIS ITEM WAS FOUND BEHIND A BOOKSHELF IN AN ANTIQUE BOOK STORE.

258. THIS GUY WAS ARRESTED DUE TO AN INCIDENT INVOLVING A BREADSTICK.

259. You're on vacation in Mexico. You stumble upon an ancient cavern used for human sacrifices. Draw what you see.

260. YOU PICK UP A PURSE LAYING ON THE GROUND. IT'S MOVING. DRAW WHAT'S INSIDE.

261. THIS POOR GUY JUST ATE SOME BAD MEAT. DRAW THE AFTERMATH.

262. THIS CREATURE LIVES IN THE SEWERS.

263. THE CANNIBALS ARE COMING! DRAW ONE.

264. THIS DOG HAS A STRANGE MUTATION.

265. THIS GUY'S IDEA OF A GOOD TIME IS EATING POTATO CHIPS AND WATCHING RERUNS OF OLD TV SHOWS. DRAW HIS WIFE.

266. THIS EVENT JUST RUINED THIS GIRL'S SWEET SIXTEENTH BIRTHDAY PARTY.

267. AN ODD COUPLE'S IDEA OF A GOOD TIME.

268. YOU WENT INTO THE MEN'S DEPARTMENT STORE LOOKING FOR SOCKS. YOU CAME OUT LOOKING LIKE THIS.

269.   THE STRONGEST BARBARIAN.

270.   BUSINESS IN THE FRONT. PARTY IN THE BACK.

271. IF YOU'VE GOT IT, FLAUNT IT.

272. IMAGINE YOU ARE A FAMOUS CELEBRITY. YOU'VE JUST BEEN ALERTED THAT A CRAZED FAN IS LOOSE IN YOUR HOUSE. DRAW THE FAN.

273. THIS PERSON COLLECTS AND RECYCLES CANS FOR A LIVING.

274.   A SCOTTISH HIGHLANDER.

275. AN UNDERWATER WORLD. DRAW WHAT IT LOOKS LIKE.

276. THIS GARDEN GNOME COMES ALIVE AT NIGHT.

277. A world war 2 plane found deep in the jungle.

278. A hotdog that is topped with unusual condiments.

279. THIS PERSON'S NICKNAME WAS "BIGHEAD" IN HIGH SCHOOL.

280. A NEW TYPE OF INSECT WAS FOUND IN VENEZUELA. DRAW IT.

281. SKETCH THE PLACE WHERE YOU FEEL MOST COMFORTABLE.

282. THIS TV REPAIR MAN HOOKS UP ILLEGAL CABLE.

283.   A GUILTY PLEASURE.

284.   A COLLEGE DORM ROOM.

285.   THIS POOR ANIMAL IS STUCK IN QUICKSAND.

286.   THIS GUY LOST HIS TEETH IN A STREET FIGHT.

287. A PUBLIC SCHOOL TEACHER ON THE LAST DAY OF SCHOOL.

288. THIS LADY'S EYES ARE WAY TOO CLOSE TOGETHER. DRAW HER WITH BIZARRE FACIAL FEATURES.

289. A VILLAIN'S GETAWAY VEHICLE.

290.   A WORLD FAMOUS UNDERWEAR MODEL.

291.   THE SCREENSHOT FROM A CLASSIC VIDEO GAME.

292.   SOMEONE JUST PHOTOBOMBED YOUR GRADUATION PICTURE. DRAW IT.

293.   THIS CONVICT SPENDS 21 HOURS A DAY IN SOLITARY CONFINEMENT.

294. Draw a loyal fan in the stands at a baseball game.

295. An unidentified flying object just crashed into your house. Draw the scene.

296. A SWEATY, OVERWEIGHT PERSON IN A CROWDED ELEVATOR.

297. THE GHOST THAT HAUNTS AN OLD THEATRE.

298. ONE MORE DEMERIT POINT AND THIS BUS DRIVER LOSES HIS LICENCE.

299. THIS WOMAN HAS ABSOLUTELY NO TOLERANCE FOR INSUBORDINATION.

300. YOU JUST RETURNED HOME FROM A SOCIAL GATHERING. LOOKING AT YOURSELF IN THE MIRROR YOU NOTICE SOMETHING ON YOUR FACE. WHY DIDN'T ANYONE TELL YOU IT WAS THERE? DRAW YOUR FACE.

301. THIS IS THEIR FIRST TIME AT A COUPLES YOGA CLASS.

302.   A GRIMY PIRATE WITH A LOT OF CHARACTER.

303.   AN ANIMAL IN A SPACE SUIT.

304. DRAW A TROLL LIVING UNDER A BRIDGE.

305. THIS POSTER IS OF AN 80'S PUNK ROCK BAND. DRAW THE POSTER.

306.   SOOO ILLEGAL.

307.   THIS GUY BREEDS SNAKES FOR A LIVING.

308. THIS OBSCURE RADIO HAS A SPECIAL FUNCTION. DRAW IT.

309. A GIRL GUIDE TRYING TO SELL YOU COOKIES.

310.   A SQUEEGEE KID.

311.   A HAND PUPPET THAT GIVES KIDS NIGHTMARES.

312. YOU NEVER WOULD HAVE EXPECTED TO SEE THIS IN A SPIDER'S WEB.

313. THIS GUY MADE A SUPER HERO COSTUME OUT OF THINGS LAYING AROUND THE HOUSE. LABEL THE ITEMS HE USED.

314. THESE CHICKENS LIVE ON TOP OF A COW.

315. A SINISTER LOOKING BABY.

316. A RECLUSIVE MISFIT LIVES IN THIS ABANDONED CHURCH.

317. A FRENCH GUILLOTINE IN ACTION. DRAW THE SCENE.

318. YOU SPOT SOMETHING INTERESTING WHILE SNORKELING OVER THE CORAL REEF. WHAT IS IT?

319. A REALISTIC DRAWING OF SOMETHING FROM MEMORY.

320. These people work in a factory where phone accessories are assembled.

321. A nuclear power plant.

322. YOU'VE GONE CAMPING FOR THE WEEKEND. DRAW YOUR CAMPSITE.

323. THESE CIRCUS FREAKS DRAW THE BIGGEST CROWD.

324. THIS DOLL HAS A SOUL.

325. DRAW A SCENE FROM AN EPIC BATTLE.

326. THIS KID IS SHOPLIFTING FROM A CONVENIENCE STORE.

327. THIS GIRL TALKS ON THE PHONE WAY TOO MUCH. SHE ALSO LOVES TO SHOP ONLINE.

328. A PAPER AIRPLANE LOADED WITH STICKERS AND DESIGNS.

329. A FASCINATING STATUE ON DISPLAY IN A MUSEUM.

330.   THIS GUY COLLECTS MODEL TRAINS.

331. WHAT WOULD YOU LOOK LIKE IF YOU STUCK YOUR FINGER IN A LIGHT SOCKET?

332. THIS IS THE MASCOT FOR AN UNDEFEATED VOLLEYBALL TEAM.

333. A WORM FIGHTING OFF A FISH.

334. YOU ARE WALKING DOWN THE STREET PLAYING A GAME ON YOUR PHONE. YOU END UP IN SOME UNKNOWN PART OF TOWN. DRAW WHAT YOU SEE.

335. DRAW 3 BLOBS ON YOUR PAGE. TURN THEM INTO OBJECTS.

336. AN ECCENTRIC ARCHITECT DESIGNED THIS HOUSE.

337. THIS PERSON IS EXTREMELY ANGRY.

338. SHE'S A DIVA.

339. DRAW YOUR FACIAL EXPRESSION DURING A BRAIN-FREEZE.

340. A VINTAGE AIRCRAFT AND ITS PILOT.

341.   YOU JUST REALIZED THAT YOU LOCKED YOUR KEYS IN THE CAR. THIS IS WHAT HAPPENED NEXT.

342.   THIS CHARACTER IS EXTREMELY BORED.

343. ENGAGING IN AWKWARD SMALL TALK AT THE OFFICE WATER COOLER WITH A CO-WORKER.

344. THIS HARD-CORE ANIMAL ACTIVIST WANTS CHANGE!

345. A VERY PECULIAR COSTUME PARTY.

346.   A HIPSTER'S INNER CITY GARDEN.

347.   THIS POOR THING IS MISSING SOME TEETH.

348. WHAT ARE YOU DOING WHEN YOU ARE FULLY RELAXED? DRAW IT.

349. THIS DARN DOG WON'T STOP POOPING ON THE CARPET.

350. THESE GERMS ANNIHILATED THE HUMAN RACE.

351. THIS IS WHAT HAPPENS WHEN YOU DON'T WEAR SAFETY GEAR ON THE JOB SITE.

352. DRAW A NEW LOGO FOR A BIKER GANG.

353. SATAN'S ILLEGITIMATE SON.

354. FOOD FIGHT!

355. DOING SOMETHING INAPPROPRIATE AT THE LIBRARY.

356. THE HOST OF A LATE-NIGHT TALK SHOW THAT AIRS AT 4:00 A.M.

357. YOU'RE ORDERING SOMETHING FROM THE DRIVE-THROUGH WINDOW AT A FAST FOOD RESTAURANT. DRAW THE SCENE.

358. A BELLY DANCER AT A HOOKAH BAR.

359. A BEAT-UP, UNRELIABLE DELIVERY TRUCK.

360. THESE GUYS ARE LIVING THE HIGH LIFE.

361.   A PUBLIC DISPLAY OF AFFECTION.

362.   THIS CHARACTER IS INCREDIBLY UNINTELLIGENT.

363. THIS NECKLACE WAS WORN BY A SHAMAN.

364. A MEMORY FROM YOUR DEEP SUBCONSCIOUS.

365. THE LAST PAGE IN YOUR SKETCH BOOK. SO SAD! DRAW WHAT YOU ARE GOING TO DO WITH ALL YOUR FREE TIME AFTER YOU'RE DONE.

BONUS: DRAW SOMETHING ODD ON TOP OF MY HEAD!

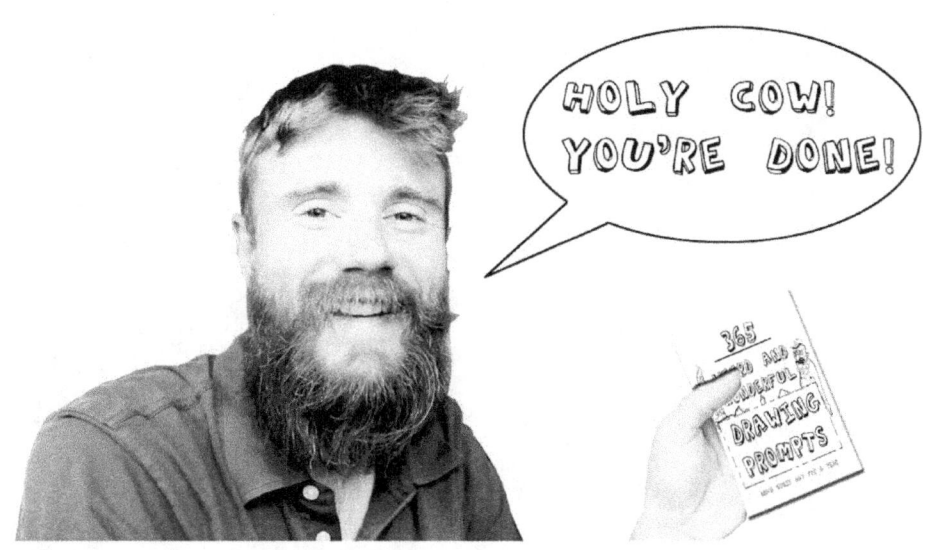

www.ingramcontent.com/pod-product-compliance
Lightning Source LLC
Chambersburg PA
CBHW082320220526
45470CB00008B/2361